Stunt
Flying

Henry Billings and Melissa Billings

Published in association with The Basic Skills Agency

Hodder & Stoughton

A MEMBER OF THE HODDER HEADLINE GROUP

Acknowledgements

Cover: Airsport Photo Library/Simon Ward

Photos: pp. 2, 8, 23 © Allsport; pp. 5, 15 © Hulton Getty;
pp. 12, 19, 26 © Corbis.

Orders: please contact Bookpoint Ltd, 130 Milton Park, Abingdon, Oxon OX14 4SB.
Telephone: (44) 01235 827720, Fax: (44) 01235 400454. Lines are open from 9.00–6.00,
Monday to Saturday, with a 24 hour message answering service.

British Library Cataloguing in Publication Data
A catalogue record for this title is available from The British Library

ISBN 0 340 86947 X

Published by Jamestown Publishers,
a division of NTC/Contemporary Publishing Group, Inc.

First published in UK 1999 by Hodder & Stoughton Educational Publishers.
This edition published 2002
Impression number   10 9 8 7 6 5 4 3 2 1
Year   2006 2005 2004 2003 2002

Typeset by Fakenham Photosetting Ltd, Fakenham, Norfolk.
Printed in Great Britain for Hodder & Stoughton Educational, a division of Hodder Headline
Plc, 338 Euston Road, London NW1 3BH by The Bath Press Ltd.

Charles Hamilton was no fool.
'We shall all be killed
if we stay in the business,' he said.
Hamilton was lucky.
He ended up dying a natural death.
But many of his friends
died in balls of flames.

What 'business' was Hamilton in?
He was a stunt flyer.
He and other daredevil pilots
thrilled fans with their
high-risk moves in the sky.

Watching a stunt flyer beats a trip to the circus.

It all began around 1910 in America.
Aviation, or flying aircraft, was new.
Many people were excited
just to see a plane.
And when that plane started doing tricks
it was better than a trip to the circus.
In fact, that was what stunt pilots
called their acts: flying circuses.

One of the first great stunt pilots
was an American called Lincoln Beachey.
He could do amazing things
in the flimsy planes of the day.
He could, for instance,
pick a handkerchief off the airfield
with his wingtip.

In 1911 Beachey stunned people
when he flew under the bridge
at Niagara Falls.
But his boldest stunt
was to fly straight up
until he ran out of fuel.
Then, somehow,
he glided his 'dead' plane back to earth.

Lincoln Beachey was one of the first stunt pilots.

In 1912 Beachey got a call
from a man who made aeroplanes.
He wanted to sell his planes
to the US Army.
But the Army did not think
that the planes could do
a tight figure of eight in the sky.
So he asked Beachey
to fly a demonstration.
Beachey flew a tighter figure of eight
than anyone had ever seen.

The next day, some men from the Army
asked Beachey a favour.
They asked him never to fly
on a US Army airfield again.
The reason?
They were worried that their own pilots
would try to copy Beachey's stunt
and get killed.

Stunt flying is a dangerous sport.

Instead, it was Beachey who got killed.
It happened in 1915
while he was doing an air show.
During a difficult trick,
the wings on his plane broke.
Over fifty thousand fans watched in horror
as Beachey's plane span out of control
and crashed.

Even though there were disasters,
people kept coming back for more.

Air shows really took off
after World War I ended in 1918.
The US Army had trained lots of pilots.
Suddenly, these men had nothing to do.
Many bought their own planes
and became stunt flyers.
Planes were cheap in those days
and with the war over
there were plenty for sale.

The most popular model
was a double-winged plane
called a Jenny.
It was designed to carry two people.
Pilots said
this plane could land on a penny.
They flew their Jennies from town to town,
putting on air shows.

They used open farm fields
for landing and taking off.
At night, they put their planes
into nearby barns for shelter.
These men,
plus a few equally bold women pilots,
became known as 'barnstormers'.

Double-winged planes were the most popular.

People flocked to see the air shows.
Many of the stunts
were truly death defying.
Pilots flew upside down.
They did loops close to the ground.
Sometimes a pilot took along a partner
who jumped out of the plane
in the middle of the show.
To fans who didn't know
what a parachute was,
this came as a real shock!

As the years went by,
air shows grew more and more daring.
Pilots began working with 'wing-walkers'.

These people did all sorts of crazy things
on the wings of planes.
One woman danced on the upper wing.
Another often 'fell off' a wing.
She would save herself
by grabbing a cord hanging from the plane.
Then she would place the cord
between her teeth
and begin to spin around.
People always gasped
when they saw this Iron Jaw Spin.

Gladys Roy walked the wings blindfold.

Another stunt flyer amazed crowds
by hanging from a wing by his toes.
One day he really stunned his fans.
He climbed to the top wing.
Then the pilot went into a steep dive
and ended in a full loop.
All this time, the stunt flyer
stayed standing on the wing.
A hidden cable held him in place.
But for a few moments,
the crowd felt sure
he would plunge to his death.

The fact that some pilots
did fall to their deaths
added to the thrill.

One US pilot fell out of her cockpit
during a loop.
She was more than one thousand feet
in the air at the time.
She did not survive the fall.

Sometimes two pilots would team up.
With two planes in the air,
wing-walkers could really go wild.

One woman, known as the Flying Witch,
had a daring trick.
She would climb down a rope ladder
from one plane,
then jump to the wing of a second plane.
That act was later banned, however,
when a man was killed trying to perform it.

This stunt flyer is changing to another plane. He was killed when the planes hit each other.

By 1930, air shows were dying out.
New laws against low-level flying
forced many shows to close.
Besides, flying was now seen
as serious business.
Pilots took on new challenges.

One started out as a barnstormer.
But in 1924 he became a US army pilot.
Three years later,
he made the first flight
across the Atlantic Ocean.

Another American spent years
in a flying circus.
Then he turned to long-distance flight.
In 1931 he made the first non-stop trip
across the Pacific.

Still, the attraction of stunt flying
never completely died.
In recent years,
air shows have been performed again.
Now most shows feature jets, not Jennies.
But the element of danger remains.

In 1988 German pilots held a big air show.
Pilots in nine jets
traced a big heart across the sky.
A tenth pilot
tried to draw a line of smoke
straight through the figure.
It was supposed to be an arrow
piercing the heart.
But the tenth jet didn't move fast enough.
It hit one of the other planes,
causing them both to crash to the ground.
Forty-nine people died.

Wing-walkers perform on old-style planes.

Another flyer in the US had a near miss
in a 1991 air show.
He liked to perform a trick
on an old-fashioned, double-winged plane.
He hung from a bar below the plane.
He moved his legs
as though walking in mid-air.

One day, though,
his hands slipped off the bar.
He fell ten feet
before the harness he was wearing caught him.
He dangled helplessly from the harness,
having no way to get back up to the bar.
The pilot had to drop him
onto a speeding truck
in order to save his life.

In 1991 a woman stunt flyer
found a way to combine stunt flying
and long-distance flying.
She set a new record for the longest flight
made upside down.
She flew her biplane that way
for four hours and 38 minutes.
She covered 658 miles.

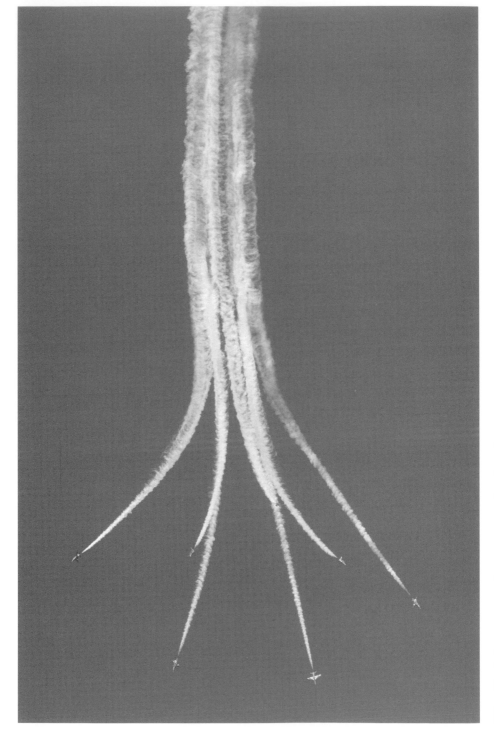

The Red Arrows make patterns in the sky.

In Britain, the famous Red Arrows
are the stunt flyers of today.
The nine-jet team was formed in 1965
and appears at air shows all over the world.

The Red Arrows perform daring stunts
in their jets.
Sometimes, the jets fly upside down
with smoke streaming from their engines.
Or they fly in front of each other,
making criss-cross patterns in the sky.
They can also roll over and over
at the same time
without losing their place in the pattern.

The Red Arrows pilots train for a long time
to do these stunts
and other pilots treat them with respect.
One said:
'They are the best.
We will not see better in our lifetime.'

Clearly, these recent events,
and others like them,
show that the sport of stunt flying
is alive and well in the world today.